# How to Have Great Meetings

## A Lean Coffee Book

### Adam Yuret

Copyright © 2016 by Adam Yuret

All rights reserved. This book or any portion thereof may not be reproduced or used in any manner whatsoever without the express written permission of the publisher except for the use of brief quotations in a book review.

Printed in the United States of America

First Printing, July 2016

ISBN:13-9781535171489

Context Driven Agility Press

www.ContextDrivenAgility.com

# Table of Contents

Introduction: A Gathering of People ............................................. i

Chapter 1: How To Lean Coffee ..................................................... 1

Chapter 2: Effective Uses of Lean Coffee ................................... 12

Chapter 3: Why Lean Coffee Works ............................................ 17

Chapter 4: Facilitation Patterns .................................................. 20

Chapter 5: When Not to Have a Meeting at All! ....................... 26

Chapter 6: Let's Love Working Together Again! ....................... 29

# Introduction

# A Gathering of People

## meeting
*noun*

**Simple Definition of MEETING**  Popularity: Top 40% of words

: a gathering of people for a particular purpose (such as to talk about business)

: a gathering of people for religious worship

: a situation or occasion when two people see and talk to each other

Source: Merriam-Webster's Learner's Dictionary

I hate "meetings". An engineer at a client I was working with recently said to me... "You know most of us engineers hate meetings, you probably love them though." She had made the logical assumption that because I am a consultant who works in strategy and leadership I must love sitting in boring rooms listening to someone prattle on endlessly about things which do not matter to me. This was how I defined "meetings" for most of my career. That is until I wandered into a coffee shop to attend my first Lean Coffee in Seattle on the recommendation of a respected colleague one early morning in 2011. That meeting and the things I've learned at Lean Coffee have meaningfully shaped my career since. I've facilitated literally hundreds of Lean Coffee sessions in the ensuing years.

My goal when working with clients is to help companies build improved capabilities and leave them to manage their own systems. The initiatives I encourage sometimes survive my departure and sometimes they don't. The contribution that has persisted more consistently than any other is the meeting and collaboration technique

"Lean Coffee," which I describe in this book. From small startups to founders of the hottest IPOs, to incumbent fortune 500's, Lean Coffee, as described here, has made meetings and collaboration awesome across a multitude of contexts.

The single most universally maligned institution in business seems to be that of the meeting. People are summoned via electronic calendar to appear at a room where they're talked at about something irrelevant to them for a period of time.

Seldom do people see these meetings as essential work that adds value for themselves or customers (with the rare exception of the person who called the meeting). It also seems like the higher up you are in an org chart the more likely you are to be spending most, if not all, of your life in these meetings.

Talking with each other is the most important thing we do. Not just because communication is vital to working together effectively but also because we're social animals. Having real personal relationships with people makes us more effective at achieving the outcomes we endeavor to pursue together.

Meetings enjoy their current bad reputation in part because we've tried to optimize them for the wrong things. We only meet with each other when we want to disseminate information, usually in one direction only. When a team or individuals are falling short of our expectations of them we call a meeting. I've even seen meetings called to chastise an entire organization for the perceived poor performance of a few.

When engineers are compelled to attend an informational meeting the agenda of which is to inform them they are not productive they quite logically begin to question whether or not meeting helped them to become so. Sadly the long duration and unpleasantness of these meetings creates a culture where those in the meeting have only one goal: to escape the meeting as soon as possible. This actually further exacerbates the problem in that no genuine dialog can occur because if you speak, you risk prolonging the pain. Unfortunately, meetings are often misused and formatted in such a way that very few attendees actually get to participate in them.

> *"I guarantee people will stop complaining about meetings when you let them actually start to participate in them."*
>
> — *Jeff Patton (Author of "User Story Mapping", Agile Roots 2015)*

In my work I often encounter organizations struggling to communicate effectively. Consequently, I find myself recommending meaningful ways to optimize face-to-face collaboration. I advocate for replacing many painful meeting types with less painful non-meeting alternatives. My purpose in writing this book is not just to give examples of when not to have meetings, but to introduce the "Lean Coffee" framework for effective meetings. I've facilitated literally hundreds of these meetings in dozens of contexts at every level of every size organizations, from the Fortune 5 to small, local community gatherings, from executives to engineers. I've seen passionate engagement from participants and more effective decision-making in Lean Coffee meetings, so much so that I want to share the framework with the world.

All of this is only possible because Jim Benson (Modus Cooperandi) and Jeremy Lightsmith founded this rich and thriving Seattle Lean Coffee community of practice and format in 2009.

Thanks to their innovation we can finally stop suffering and start enjoying working together effectively.

# Chapter 1: How To Lean Coffee

*Alone we can do so little; together we can do so much.*

— *Helen Keller*

### Lean Coffee has Seven Basic Steps:

1. Set up the meeting table (< 1 minute)
2. Introduce how Lean Coffee works (< 2 minutes)
3. Invite attendees to introduce themselves (*optional)
4. Invite attendees to introduce their topics
5. Vote on the topics
6. Begin timeboxed discussion
7. Invite takeaways

## 1. Set up the Meeting Table

Set up the table, creating a rudimentary visual board using four sticky notes (see Figure 1-1). Place sticky notes and pens all around the table and invite people to write topics on the sticky notes and stick them in the "Topics" column.

A rudimentary visual board consisting of four columns is created using sticky notes nearest to the center of the table.

Tip: Use the table because a white board might discourage people from walking up to propose topics.

**Figure 1-1**

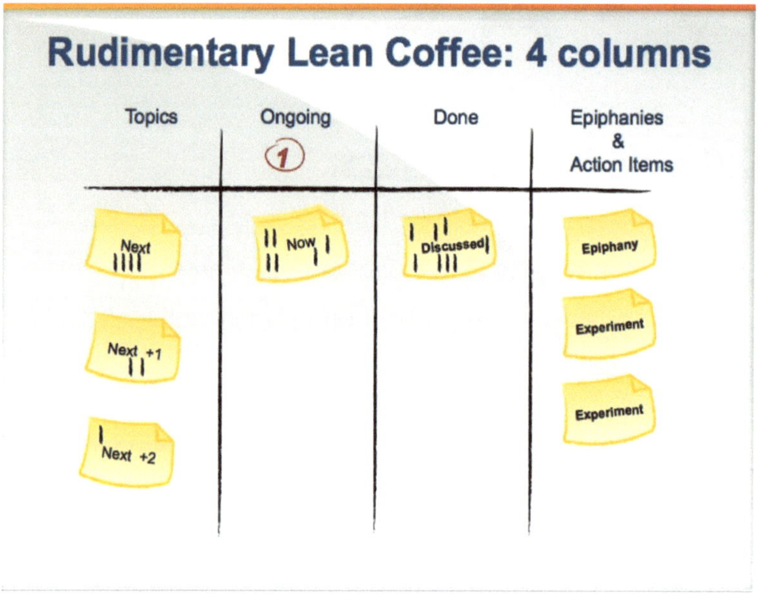

**Rudimentary Lean Coffee: 4 columns**

| Topics | Ongoing | Done | Epiphanies & Action Items |
|---|---|---|---|
| Next | Now | Discussed | Epiphany |
| Next +1 | | | Experiment |
| Next +2 | | | Experiment |

## 2. Introduce How Lean Coffee Works

Some people will be first-timers to the Lean Coffee meeting. A quick run-down of the concepts (like where the exits are and how to put on a life vest) should be shared. For example, I usually say:

"Lean Coffee asks everyone to contribute topic ideas. We can add topics any time, but during our quick opening round of introductions is a good time to think about and add topics. Nobody is compelled to contribute a topic. Once we've introduced ourselves, we'll ask each contributor to elaborate on his or her topic in one or two quick sentences. After each contributor has elaborated on their topics, we will then individually vote on them (each person gets two votes) and then discuss the highest voted topic first in a timeboxed fashion. The way the timebox works is we set a timer for 5 minutes. When the chime sounds nobody has to stop talking. We silently Roman vote, thumbs-up or thumbs-down, and if we have a majority of up votes we'll check again every three minutes or until the group decides to move onto the next topic. A few minutes before our meeting is over we'll gather takeaways from people to learn what they got out of this meeting and, if applicable, what they will do next."

You don't need to cover all eventualities, people will watch and learn.

## 3. Invite Attendees to Introduce Themselves

Sometimes people meeting for Lean Coffee don't know each other. Asking each person to introduce themselves with one or two quick sentences, to let folks around the table know who they are and from where they're coming, can be a good thing to do while people are writing down topics.

## 4. Invite Attendees to Introduce Their Topics

Ask the contributor of each topic to give a two-sentence description so that everyone understands the topic before they vote. As a facilitator, be on your toes here, just enough to make the sticky note topic clear. Often people are so excited to discuss that they just want to launch into the topic. If this happens a polite suggestion to vote on the topic when the time comes is usually well received.

## 5. Vote on the Topics

Typically everyone is given two votes to place on whatever topic they'd like (See figure 1-1). They can put two votes on their own topic if that reflects their passion best.

## 6. Begin Timeboxed Discussion

Pull the most popular topic and move the note into the ongoing column, set the time (five minutes initially and three subsequently), Roman-vote, and majority rules. When the majority decides to move onto a new topic allow the speaker to finish their thought, move the topic to the done column and proceed. It is essential that the value of the conversation trumps all other things. If the whole group votes down but continues to actively discuss, the behavior trumps the downvote rule and another minute should be added to the timer.

## 7. Invite Takeaways

Minutes before the meeting is scheduled to end go around the table and gather takeaways. A takeaway consists of one or two sentences describing the value each person will be taking away from the meeting. Nobody is compelled to share a takeaway; anyone is free to simply say "pass". A takeaway needn't be laudatory; it is just as useful to express a criticism and/or suggestion for future improvement.

## Why is it called Lean Coffee?

The name Lean Coffee originates from the original intent to create a community of practice around lean thinking in Seattle and, since it started in a coffee shop, "Lean Coffee" made logical sense.

Of course as a methodology this name is not entirely descriptive as the meeting needn't be about lean principles nor does it have to offer or discuss coffee. Some organizations call them "lean meetings" or "pop-up kanban" meetings. Call it whatever you like, as long as meetings stop sucking and start being a great place to learn and collaborate.

## Why is Lean Coffee worth doing?

- Engagement: Helps cover the most important topics to the majority of people first.
- Focus: Stops one topic taking the whole meeting.
- Efficiency: Allows the group to move on when they have enough understanding to proceed.
- Egalitarian: Captures what's on people's minds (even the topics you don't cover) so that everyone is heard and even if their topic is not discussed, follow-up can happen after the meeting.
- Clarity: Real time feedback by the room (and a regular timer alarm) helps people limit their ramblings. The meeting is engaging or it is over.

One of the most common things I hear from people who attend meetings is: "I was so bored in that meeting and could not have cared less about the topics covered." The people running those meetings on the other hand often say, "Nobody was paying attention! Now we'll need to have more of these meetings so people get the information!" as though repeating the same behavior will produce a different result.

People being summoned are not interested in the meeting and people doing the summoning hate this.

The main strength of Lean Coffee is group prioritization of ideas and topics. This shared responsibility to create the agenda for the meeting, and then support group management of the duration of and engagement in each topic has powerful impact.

## The Mechanics of Lean Coffee

The way Lean Coffee works is by applying a minimal level of constraints and creating an egalitarian environment that supports collaboration.

At least one person helps the group effectively optimize for value and ensures that any straying from the rules is intentional and made explicit facilitates Lean Coffee. The facilitator(s) is also responsible for paying attention to the weak signals around the table in order to ensure a smooth interaction among the participants. We will cover in greater detail the role of Lean Coffee facilitator in chapter three.

Tip: The facilitator is not the 'leader' of the meeting. They are not the arbiter of value or enforcer of the rules. They are there to help the group do what the group wants to do. Empathy and attention to weak signals is essential and a light touch required. If a single person aggressively manages a Lean Coffee meeting, it becomes a regular meeting and dies.

As with many Lean tools, Lean Coffee is deceptively simple. The tools are simple: a table, sticky notes and sharpie markers (or any writing utensil). A round table is ideal, but any surface will do. The pads of sticky notes and writing utensils are spread around the table so that all participants can easily reach them. We've run out of sticky notes and used napkins before.

The rules of Lean Coffee are intentionally kept minimal and flexible, but they are essential to the success of Lean Coffee meetings. When people arrive they're encouraged to suggest topics to discuss pertaining to a theme that is defined, usually implicitly by the surrounding context and sometimes explicitly by organizers. Topics are suggested by writing them on the ubiquitous sticky notes and sticking the proposed topics under the table/board's "Ready" column.

After a brief round of introductions, the topics are described in brief by each proposer. We often suggest keeping the descriptions brief using a "roughly two-sentence" rule of thumb. Given the strong engagement often enabled by this format, people are usually eager to jump into discussion during this stage.

Brevity at this stage is important but that doesn't mean stifling all interaction. If a question needs answering in order to understand of the topic, it should be asked. The tricky part is identifying the line between clarifying questions and premature group interaction on a topic. The main reason to avoid ad-hoc discussion during the clarification process is because the group has not yet been given an opportunity to learn about the topics they're giving up by engaging in this discussion.

Once the group agrees that shared understanding of the topics available has been achieved there is a quick vote. Voting consists of putting a mark on the topic you're most interested in discussing. The number of votes permitted is limited to two or three per person. Again this is a heuristic, not a rigid rule, however, after several years and over a hundred Lean Coffees, I've observed the third vote almost always feels like a throw away vote.

People seem to have a strong first and second choice, but third choices are more difficult to pin down. As with all of these rules, I encourage experimentation and adaptation to your context.

Once the votes are tallied the timeboxed discussion begins with the most popular topic. The sticky note is moved into the "Doing" column and a timer is started. In the event of a tie the facilitator chooses a topic at random.

The timebox is intended to itself be a minimally invasive constraint. Its purpose is to allow for a regular check of the group's interest in the subject. A timer is set for an initial timebox of five minutes and the proposer of the topic is invited to kick off the discussion.

When the timer goes off, an unobtrusive alarm signals the silent Roman vote (See figure 1-2). Nobody needs to stop interacting when this happens; in fact participants are explicitly instructed at the start that the vote should not interrupt flow.

The silent Roman vote merely consists of holding one's thumb up to signify interest in the current topic. Thumbs up signals an interest to proceed with another reduced three-minute timebox. Thumbs horizontal indicates ambivalence. Thumbs down is not a negative or critical signal, it just expresses an interest in discussing the next topic or a lack of anything further to contribute to the current one.

**Figure 1-2 - The Roman Vote**

"I want to keep talking about this!"

"I'm ready to move to the next topic."

"I'm ambivalent about continuing this topic."
(Also known as the "Minnesota Down Vote")

In the event of a majority up vote the facilitator will set another timebox about half the length of the first one (e.g. three minutes) and then repeat the process every three minutes until there are a majority of down votes, at which time the current topic is moved to the "Done" column and the next one is moved to the "Doing" column.

When the time set aside for the meeting is about to elapse (usually leaving about 30 seconds per participant at the end) the group is invited to share "Takeaways". Takeaways are meant to be a brief description of the value received by each participant. It's an opportunity for people to share not only what they got out of the experience, but to also share suggestions for improvements in the process or actions they might take based on the discussion. Participants may also opt to "pass" if they choose.

Lean Coffee meetings are typically most effective when at least 90 minutes is dedicated to them. An hour can still be effective, but less than an hour usually leaves insufficient time for an effective conversation. While it always depends on the group dynamic three hours is a decent maximum for a Lean Coffee. Even at three hours I think taking a break halfway through is a good idea, if for no other reason to allow people to move their bodies around and refresh their minds.

Group size impacts any meeting. Sometimes a small group of people with little in common will have an ineffective gathering whoreas a large group, well facilitated with common interests, will have an awesome meeting. As a rule we've found that approximately 14 people is the maximum for highly effective Lean Coffee meetings. I've facilitated excellent Lean Coffee sessions with forty people and had challenging meetings with four. As a rule if there are more than 14 people before starting, I recommend splitting into two meetings. Instead of doing takeaways at each table, bring the groups together to share each table's respective takeaways and topics as a closing.

## Chapter 2: Effective Uses of Lean Coffee

*"Our greatest strength lies in collaboration, not competition."*

— *Joseph Rain*

### Sensemaking

Understanding what's really happening in our organization is difficult. Most communication channels are either limited by a predefined scope and therefore audience, or lack safety to express views openly.

A recurring Lean Coffee, where people from across the organization are invited to meet and discuss topics that are meaningful and important to them, can be an incredibly powerful and effective way to surface issues. It also creates a forum where various parts of an organization that would ordinarily never interact can share information and approaches to solve problems. I've facilitated Lean Coffee with every one of my clients and it has been universally regarded as a highly effective and useful means of sharing concerns across an organization.

When you ask people to write the topics they're currently interested in talking about on sticky notes, even the most introverted voices seem to feel comfortable speaking out in a room full of people. Often, the introverts' topics get the most votes, removing all doubt about the importance of the topic.

Having leadership present for Lean Coffee can add an empowering element in that, when concerns are surfaced, the people with the agency to solve those problems outside the team's control are on hand to help. Often when this happens, we'll start the subsequent Lean Coffee with a check-in on how the problem is resolving since the previous Lean Coffee.

## Retrospectives

Agile teams using the Scrum framework are familiar with the concept of the sprint retrospective. Whether your team is doing scrum, or any agile framework or not, retrospectives can be a powerful tool for improvement.

A great source of information on how to have effective retrospectives is Esther Derby and Diana Larsen's excellent book: "Agile Retrospectives: Making Good Teams Great"

Esther and Diana outline the five steps to effective retrospectives as:

1. Set the stage.
2. Gather data.
3. Generate insights.
4. Decide what to do.
5. Close the retrospective.

{1}Derby, Esther; Larsen, Diana (2006-07-26). Agile Retrospectives: Making Good Teams Great (Pragmatic Programmers) (Kindle Locations 256-258). Pragmatic Bookshelf.

Lean Coffee Retrospectives (Mapped to the retrospective framework):

1. Introductions at Lean Coffee and Topic Generation
2. Sharing topics with the group
3. Discussing the topics and gathering epiphanies
4. Choosing an experiment from the actionable epiphanies gathered
5. Takeaways

**Figure 2-1**

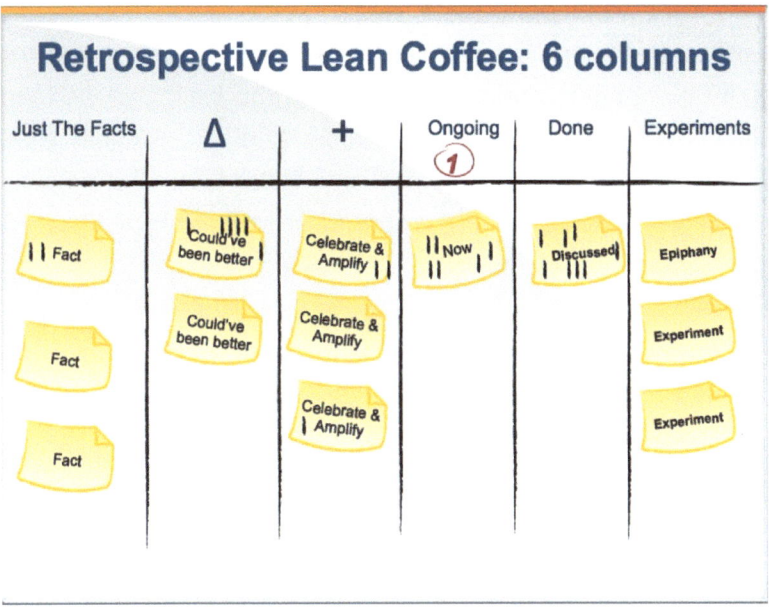

In a retrospective, the team gathers to discuss value that has recently been delivered, and seeks to understand that which enabled or impeded delivery of that value.

The purpose of the retrospective is not simply to complain or celebrate but to identify areas of potential improvement, which could make the team more effective at delivering value in the future.

The output of a retrospective meeting should be a small number of experiments (one is a good heuristic starting point) that the team agrees to execute during the course of the next cycle. These experiments are to be revisited no later than at the subsequent retrospective.

## How Can Lean Coffee Help with Retrospectives?

Lean Coffee can provide a structure that facilitates conversation about the work we've done and how it impacted our delivery of value. By creating a column for substantive things that went well "+", a column for things to improve "Δ", and a column for things we learned, we're able to create a pool of possible subjects for the group to discuss. Voting happens just as in any other Lean Coffee meeting and, if the team chooses to focus solely on one of these three categories, then that's the value the team hopes to get out of the discussion.

Everything else follows the Lean Coffee model, with the exception that a greater focus should be on coming away with at least one experiment for the team to try. At the end of Lean Coffee, just before takeaways, the team should vote on which experiments to tackle. I recommend limiting votes for the experiment to one vote per team member. The team should decide how many experiments it has bandwidth to tackle in the next cycle and then plan on executing the most popular experiments.

## Training

Training is also a gathering of people and therefore fits our definition of a meeting. The tricky bit about training is the bias to present a pre-defined syllabus to the class. I find training is more effective when the class is involved in not only what they're going to learn, but how they'll learn it. Training is also more engaging and fun for all involved when the manner in which the training will be delivered is decided by the group being trained.

Typically, when I train teams I'll hand over the training to them by facilitating the creation of a learning objectives backlog for the team. We'll encourage people to write down topics about which they'd like to learn more and put them in a backlog. Then the team votes and chooses a timebox for segments (usually between twenty and ninety minutes) of that training (usually the time leading up to the next break).

We then use the Roman vote and timeboxes to check with the class about how satisfied they are with what they've learned so far. If we get a majority of down votes I check with the upvotes about what they feel has been left out. If the down-voters are moved to cover those specific aspects of the topic then we'll continue until the majority are satisfied sufficiently to move on. If we decide to move on, I'll summarize what we covered in that time, highlight a few options of what we may pursue another time and seek takeaways from the class before we break and then tackle the next subject.

When I've used this training method, I have had participants tell me that they liked being in control of the material direction and duration.

# Chapter 3: Why Lean Coffee Works

*"If you had to identify, in one word, the reason why the human race has not achieved, and never will achieve, its full potential, that word would be 'meetings.'"*

— Dave Barry

One of the fundamental fallacies in traditional management is that people need to be directed in order to do the right thing. Another one is that people don't know what's happening around them. Lean Coffee turns this thinking on its head by not only putting people in charge of the duration of the meeting, but of the agenda as well. I've commonly facilitated Lean Coffees that included both teams and executives, where the executives learned that they were fundamentally mistaken about the real problems that their organization faced. That perspective can be very hard to come by and has always been appreciated by, not only those executives, but by the team members who are getting an often-rare opportunity to communicate with them.

People don't hate meetings; they hate being forced to waste their time on meaningless things that don't matter to them. Unfortunately, when one person dictates how a group of people will spend their time, the people being subjugated to that event often feel resentful. They end up spending their time stewing quietly over the stuff that matters and why they're not attending to it, rather than engaging in the meeting that's been forced upon them.

## Voices are Heard

Lean Coffee works because everybody's voice is heard. Even if somebody proposes a topic, which subsequently receives no votes, they've expressed themselves and, in doing so, taken the idea out of their head and put it into the open. When people don't vote on it the person proposing the unpopular topic gets a clear signal that there are other things more important to the group to discuss. One might think that this would lead to lots of resentment but I've never seen it happen that way in practice. In fact, I often observe that people will propose topics that they feel are important but, after seeing what other people have proposed, they realize that another person's topic is more important, so much so that they opt for that topic over their own.

## Collaborative Fixation

The silent gathering of the topics by people prevents something called collaborative fixation. If we hear somebody say something, we think about that thing. Once we think about that thing, we become unconsciously fixated on it. Studies have shown that when we hear other people's ideas it's very difficult to come up with our own divergent ideas which are not influenced by them.{1} The result of this unconscious fixation is a lack of diverse ideas. In this case there's a high probability of a homogeneous set of options from which to choose. Good brainstorming and effective gathering of diverse ideas requires silence at first and then group description of those topics.

## "Just-In-Time" Commitment

The Roman vote is often used in meetings because it is so effective at keeping the conversation on track. If we're checking every five minutes to ensure that people still care about what is being discussed, nobody will feel as though a meeting is being dominated by one person, or is wasting the group's time. We're not promising to spend an hour talking about one thing regardless of whether or not people care about that thing. Sometimes a single topic merits the entire Lean Coffee. There is no obligation to finish all topics or even one topic in the time allotted. Very few Lean Coffees ever finish the backlog of topics.

The meetings can end early or not happen at all. What if people get through the topics before the time allotted for the meeting is up? The meeting is over. Quickly gather takeaways and don't waste another minute in a meeting that has run its course. What if nobody proposes topics? This rarely happens (in fact, in groups large enough to have Lean Coffee I've never once seen it happen) but if it did happen then the meeting is cancelled. The people gathered have decided not to talk to each other. When that happens, it's essential that those people are not forced to stay, as this can lead to resentment.

Ultimately, trusting people to take pride in their work while giving them minimally-structured space in which to communicate and tools to improve will pay greater dividends than any form of control we might attempt to exert. Lean Coffee works because it provides people with a place where they know their judgment matters. They're respected as people to do the right thing and be professionals who do great work.

{1}Smith, S. M., Ward, T. B., & Schumacher, J. S. (1993). Constraining effects of examples in a creative generation task. Memory & Cognition, 21, 837–845.

## Chapter 4: Facilitation Patterns

*"When the best leader's work is done, the people will say 'we did it ourselves.'"*

*— Lao Tsu*

### What Happens when Lean Coffee Doesn't Work?

Lean Coffee is not a fixed process. Like all processes involving people it should adapt to context and grow to fit the people that it is serving. I believe that facilitation with a live human being is the best way to run a Lean Coffee. What follows are some examples, where I've seen facilitation go well and where I've seen it go wrong.

I've facilitated hundreds of Lean Coffee meetings and in that time I've learned the following things about facilitation:

- The primary job of the facilitator is to help the group get what the group wants out of the meeting.
- Detecting weak signals is the primary responsibility of the facilitator. Weak signals are those small, almost undetectable gestures people make during a conversation. Somebody leans in as if to begin speaking but nobody notices in the heat of discussion, for example. As the facilitator, the most challenging thing about weak signal detection is that it's not natural to look around a table at people who are far from the focus of the conversation. It's even less natural to interrupt on that person's behalf. When I see somebody lean in (or otherwise signal) I'll try to make eye contact with him or her and acknowledge that I've seen their intent and at the next opportunity I'll interject with their name. "Mark seemed to want to say something." Sometimes Mark will say "Oh no, I'm good." I've never seen anybody become offended by a facilitator interjecting on

another's behalf, especially when the other person's name is being used to interject.
- Facilitators in most Lean Coffees I've attended participate in the discussion. The ideal facilitator would be focused solely on facilitation. However, hiring a full time Lean Coffee facilitator is not usually in the budget. Forcing an interested team member to not participate is usually unfair to that person.

## No Facilitator/Group Facilitation

Holding Lean Coffee with no facilitator or with group facilitation can work well when you have a strong collaborative and conscientious group of people that seek weak signals and support one another. If the conversation is flowing well, people are making space for others to contribute and friction is minimal, a designated facilitator may not be needed. Even if there is a designated facilitator in these situations, their presence will go unnoticed. It's a good idea for a facilitator to seek to go unnoticed; after all, it's not about you.

## Single Facilitator

Unfortunately, it is far too easy for a single facilitator to assume a dictatorial role and this must not be allowed to occur. Once a dictator 'takes charge' Lean Coffee is dead. Often times the dictator causes so much chaos and consternation that the group/system won't tolerate it.

I've seen brilliant single facilitators pay close attention, create space and allow group members to speak and interact autonomously. I've also seen facilitators take over and use aggressive body language, or enforce the rules of Lean Coffee so stringently that ordinarily mild-mannered individuals yell profanities at the facilitator. Let me be completely clear: if somebody yells at you and you're the facilitator, it is your fault. In some ways the facilitator should be like a good game show host; essential to the seamless operation of the enterprise but invisible to an outside spectator. I don't claim to have achieved mastery of this skill as it requires continuous attention to improvement opportunities and openness to participant feedback.

Ultimately, there needs to be an understanding that anybody is welcome to facilitate the session and the reason there is a sole facilitator is because the group wishes it to be so.

## Anti-patterns

Lean Coffee is a complex system because it is a loosely coupled and dynamic interaction of people. Consequently, the number of constraints and the ways in which they are applied are very consequential to the success of the enterprise. The following two stories are extreme real examples of misapplication of constraints and the resulting dysfunctions:

## Anti-pattern #1: Too Many Rules

An anti-pattern I've see in facilitation circles is what I call "the valiant defense of the introvert." There is sometimes a belief that in every group there is at least a minority population of marginalized introverts, who, apart from being naturally insightful (because not speaking means great insight, right?), is suffering from their introversion. Where this belief is held many facilitation rules seem to be centered on an assumption that introverts are eager to be thrust into the spotlight if only the domineering extroverts would stand aside.

One such pattern is sometimes called "The Talking Stick". If somebody wants to speak they signal with a hand signal (I won't get into the weirdness of specific hand signals which are purportedly somehow less aggressive than hand-raising) and when the time comes for that person to speak they have the floor. They may not speak until they're "called on" and, in some more pernicious adaptations of this process, people are called on in clockwise order from the person currently speaking regardless of when they raised their hands or crossed their fingers or did a hokey pokey to signal their intent.

When I've seen this approach used, the exact opposite of the desired effect was the result. I never had someone (introvert or otherwise) come to me after a Lean Coffee and tell me they felt excluded until a pattern intended to include introverts was added. One attendee (who, incidentally, was not especially introverted) approached me afterward to ask me to oppose that pattern if it's ever presented again, because she literally didn't get an opportunity to speak during the entire 90 minutes.

In fact one very extroverted participant, when faced with this pattern, simply made the hand-signal and began jotting down in a notebook a backlog of things to say. Once it was that person's turn to speak he started at the top of his personal backlog (which was already out of context due to the passage of time) and worked his way down from top to bottom. Of course the time-box reduces the cost of this mistake in that before the backlog is consumed the group downvotes and we move to the next topic. Still, opportunity cost is absorbed by the group in the form of a topic that ends prematurely.

Arguably the purpose of this constraint was to encourage the introverted person, who said nothing, to speak and prevent the extroverted person from dominating the conversation. In practice it had the opposite effect. She didn't get to say a word and the dominator was even more dominant than before.

The main issue with rules and constraints is that they can take away agency from the human judgment provided by a facilitator. Rules do not detect weak signals and they can constrain thinking. Thinking is constrained when we believe that our initial consensus to obeying a new rule means we're not permitted to question that decision when we discover that rule is doing harm. As facilitator I could see that the person could not speak and that the dominator was dominating under the new rule. I had agreed with the rest of the group to abide by the new rule as an experiment, therefore I was not permitted to intervene.

The person reading off his backlog has the righteousness of having paid, with his patience, for the right to a stage and to dominate it as long as desired. After all, he's in compliance with the rules. If I said "Cathy seems to want to say something," anybody could quite rightly correct me by saying "Well, the talking stick is with Josh right now so she has to wait." I would have to either break the rule, thus risking becoming a dictator, or sit back and allow the dysfunction to persist.

## Anti-pattern #2: Too few rules

An experiment was run by a facilitator, wherein he removed what he perceived as excessive constraints: No longer did we need to limit our votes, we could add as many votes as we wanted. Of course, this was easily gamed by just putting many votes on the topic you wanted to talk about it. The conclusion was that, by offering unlimited votes, it became impossible to know that we'd be discussing the most important topic to the group. In fact the sole purpose of limiting the number of votes is to distill the passions of the people choosing.

The timer was the next thing to go. The facilitator would decide when we were done with a topic. Unfortunately, this led to a yelling incident when the facilitator misread the group. While someone was sharing an especially emotionally charged story, the facilitator leaned in and aggressively placed his hand on the sticky note in the "in progress" column, while staring at the speaker. The ordinarily mild-mannered speaker lashed out at the facilitator, "You are acting like you think you're my f**king dad!" and, with that, order was restored to the universe and the timer was reinstated

Rules are useful in the right amount. Too many rules constrain freedom and thinking while too few rules can lead to chaos. No human system will tolerate either condition for long. Ensuring that you're evolving meetings in a way that rides that fine line is essential. In fact, anybody managing people should remember that delicate balance and focus on boundaries, both explicit and tacit, and whether they're helping or hurting.

## Anti-pattern #3: Irritating Alarm

I helped run a Lean Coffee where I was remote to the group having their first Lean Coffee. The local facilitator set the alarm on his iPhone and it made the blaring loud alarm sound you'd expect to hear on a submarine that's about to dive; something as subtle as the red-alert sound in Star Trek. After the first timebox I asked the facilitator to turn down and change the tone of his alarm he agreed but did not. At the end of Lean Coffee the group was visibly annoyed and one of them said, "I hated that; the timebox for conversation was rude and I never want to do that again." That was the first and last Lean Coffee that group ever had. It's also the only Lean Coffee I've ever seen fail outright. It seems like an insignificant thing but interrupting people who are talking about things that matter to them can be a very delicate undertaking. If you enrage people they won't want to do it again. It'll just become another awful meeting. At least in the awful meetings those engineers endure on a day-to-day basis nobody puts a blaring submarine alarm on every five minutes.

# Chapter 5: When Not to Have a Meeting at All!

*"I understand that I need to focus and I'm in too many meetings. But when my assistant asks me which meetings I want to cut, I can't decide."*

— *Founder/C-level Executive*

An important part of improvement is replacing the ineffective with the effective. We can make space for Lean Coffee by eliminating the old, wasteful meetings. Let's start by exploring when not to have a meeting at all!

## Informational Meetings

Informational meetings are meetings where information is communicated from leadership to teams or status is gathered from teams by leadership.

Both of these meetings are almost always dysfunctional or at the very least unnecessary. Meetings where leaders call teams together to tell them what to do are usually one-sided affairs. Leaders seldom call such meetings to have their assumptions challenged or to hear bad news. Usually these meetings disempower teams because people doing work usually know better than leadership what needs to be done.

This can be accomplished by creating alignment across the organization regarding strategic intents. This is not a book on strategy design and deployment, so I won't detail ways to make this happen. I will tell you that it should involve a lot of passive information radiation.

An information radiator is anything which is impossible not to see that tells us important things about what is currently happening. Electronic tools are not inherently radiators of information. They can radiate information if they're clear and displayed on a big screen in an unavoidable public area.

One of the most effective information radiators is a wall with sticky notes on it. If it's clearly visible and people are encouraged to interact with it freely then it can be a very powerful tool for learning, collaboration and decision-making. Just like electronic tools, if you place this sticky note wall in a conference room somewhere removed from the people doing the work it will become a less effective radiator. In fact just moving it away from the team's workspace will transform it to an information refrigerator.

Information refrigerators are places where one has to want to seek information in order to find it. Information refrigerators do not passively convey information to people. If you have a radiator in a room everyone feels the heat. You have to want to retrieve something from the fridge in order to get it. Even opening the door of a refrigerator doesn't necessarily show you everything in it. Often you have to dig behind the moldy sandwich and pickle jars to find what you seek.

I once had an engineering director call me to task for not updating the information refrigerator with tasks I was completing. Of course I had anticipated the very moment he sent out the mandate that this would happen and had been diligently updating the tool with all of my meetings and tasks in preparation for this inevitable dressing down. He hadn't deigned to open the tool and check if I was indeed out of compliance with his mandate before calling me to task on it. In fact in that same meeting he criticized me for not having communicated a recurring meeting I was having. A meeting, which was in fact documented in the very tool he was mandating we use as our primary form of communication with him.

## Status Meetings

> *" When you ask me how long it'll take to get done, can I include status meetings in my estimate of how long it's going to take?"*
>
> — *Software Engineering Proverb*

Not only does calling groups of people into a meeting to ask them when they're going to be done disempower people, but it impedes their ability to get things done. If a meeting doesn't provide actionable information and it disempowers people, it should just be eliminated. Status meetings are one of those meetings which I strongly believe should die in a fire. If we have to ask people what they're doing that means we're not effectively communicating what is happening in our organization. This kind of information should be broadly visible everywhere we go. Teams should be able to see what's happening everywhere so they can adjust and learn. Giving teams visibility into their work and how it flows will create massive improvements in how work gets done without a single meeting taking place.

This information may lead to teams deciding to meet and have a Lean Coffee to design experiments on how to improve the things that are impeding their progress.

Alignment and Autonomy are not two ends of a spectrum; they must co-exist in order to create effective organizations. Anything that robs people of agency (the capacity, condition, or state of acting or of exerting power) drives autonomy away from alignment. People will always align to something. Leaders can choose for their people to align against mandated wasteful status meetings or for those people to solve problems and make things better for customers.

# Chapter 6: Let's Love Working Together Again!

*"Never let anyone waste your time in meaningless meetings. Except me, I get to waste your time."*

— *Anonymous VP of Engineering*
*(when people started walking away)*

There are many more useful ways to facilitate a meeting than are typically employed at organizations today. Lean Coffee is one of them but there are others. Sometimes during a Lean Coffee a product development group discovers that they're exploring feature requirements of the product they develop. A skilled and experienced facilitator knows when to say "It seems like what we're needing is to build a story map. Should we table this discussion and schedule a story-mapping session or do we have the time and people we need to just adjourn and start mapping what we want to build now?"

Sometimes only two people show up to an open meeting and it stops making sense to put sticky notes on a table and vote. When that happens, if those folks want to talk to each other, they should. If they don't want to talk to each other, then the meeting is over before it begins and that precious time is recaptured.

The main message I hope to convey with this book is the importance of communicating when working with people. If you're not communicating then you're working near people, not with them. It's easy to remember if you think of the "co" in the word "communicate" as being indicative of sharing information between people.

> *"If you're asking the 'three questions':*
>
> *- What did I do yesterday?*
> *- What do I intend to do today?*
> *- Am I blocked by anything from doing my work?*
>
> *That is a sure sign that you don't already know the answers to those questions and therefore you're not visualizing your work effectively"*
>
> — *Jim Benson*

Sadly meetings have become a catchall container for everything for which we lack an actual solution. Meetings intended to communicate day-to-day status should be replaced with passive information radiators such as big touch screens or white boards with sticky notes on them.

People don't enjoy sitting in a room listening to people tell each other what is happening on a day to day basis. People respond to the visual stimulus of a board that shows what's happening.

This single dysfunction (informational meetings) is probably the biggest cause of meeting-fatigue. If we focus meetings on valuable, necessary interactions between people working together and allow them to define what that means, we will see meetings evolve into meaningful interactions between people keenly interested in getting important things done.

Nobody hates meetings; they hate having their time wasted, being bored, being subjugated to authority for little other purpose than to be reminded of their (lower) position in the pecking order. They hate being forced to stop doing things that are meaningful to them for any of those empty reasons. People are smart and have good judgment, if they say meetings suck, they do. Understand why their meetings are terrible and invite them to the table to work out how to fix those problems.

Until we focus our attentions to creating environments where people communicate and enjoy doing so, we'll continue to suffer the misery of mandated soul-crushing meetings. Let's love work again and take back our communities.